---

This wacky idea would have never left the dock without the support of so many people.
First, I'd like to thank my wife for always supporting my outrageous ideas. Letting my passions sometimes steer our family's ship without hesitancy – As we know it's always "Family First".

To my parent's for setting the purest example of what it is to work hard whilst always being a gentleman in a world full of some scary pirates.

To my own Motley Crew "The Cresta Crew" thank you for always waiving any flag without question – helping one another.

I want to thank Devin for her talent's for not only giving this project a heartbeat but truly bringing it to Life.

Finally, I'd like to thank my kids, this book is for you. The greatest joy I have as a Dad is watching your face's light up. My imagination, determination, and motivation to support and always make you smile will never cease to exist. And if you are ever not happy...don't worry dad will be "the sneak" and get you a donut :)

Story edited by: Amir "Gorilla W." Savar

# CAPTAIN SCALLYWAG

Words by Trey Van Buskirk

Illustrations by Devin Seymour

This Legendary Tale begins

in Pineapple Port  (PIRATE TOWN)

A place so treacherous it looks like a fort

The captains, the crew,

the food and the grog

Kept everyone happy unless there was fog

The happiest of the pirates –

just so happened to be

A bird with one eye and one leg you see!

Captain Scallywag!

Captain Scallywag!

Captain Scallywag!

He would exclaim

Always trying to sell his donuts,

not for money...not for fame

Captain Scallywag knew

that his donuts would make pirates smile

Even Motley the neighborhood

Angry Pet Crocodile

His donuts however, no one cared to buy

Which left this pirate bird with

no choice but to cry

But Captain Scallywag refused to give up
He knew that people would love his
donuts, that this was just a rut

One day as he sailed through town
with a fresh batch
A fellow friend, saw him – threw a
pineapple, and said CATCH!

Off balance, woobling and wobbling

Captain Scallywag fell over

Donuts everywhere on the ground –

not one leftover

As his friend rushed over to make

sure he was ok

He was stopped in his tracks only to say

Captain Scallywag! You stepped on a

donut and now it's on your peg leg

Please, please let me help you,

don't make me beg

The donut came off to the sound of a POP!

And then quickly, immediately Captain

Scallywag said STOP!

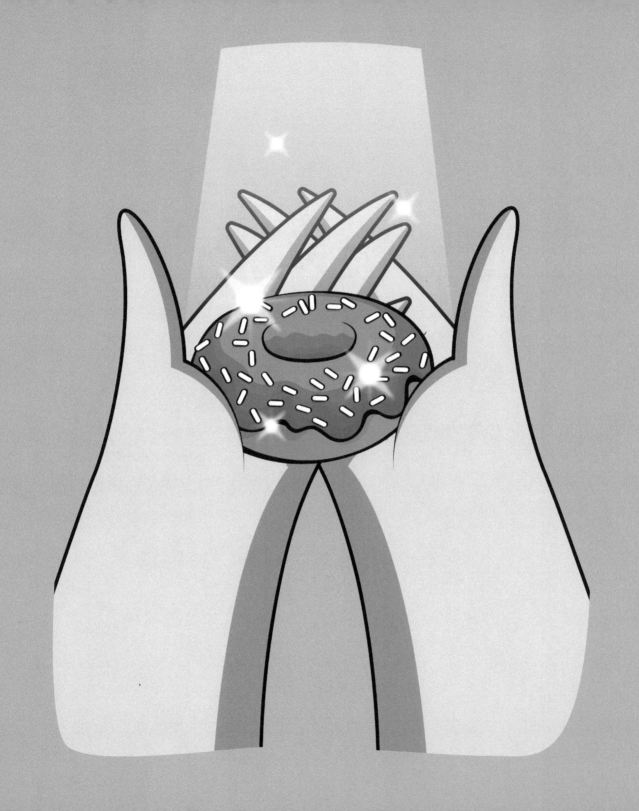

Look down, look down, look what
you've done!
There's a hole in my donut...now they
look fun!

It was from that moment on that Captain
Scallywag changed the look
Everyone now wanted a donut from the
Pineapple Port Cook!

The donut shape changed but Captain Scallywag did not
He was still the happiest pirate except now with a yacht

So remember, always smile and find
passion in what you do
Grab a Scallywag donut and don't forget
to chew!

CPSIA information can be obtained
at www.ICGtesting.com
Printed in the USA
LVHW072308210121
677169LV00026B/937

9 781087 939186